T0370020

Sleepless

IN Sangria

60 ROM-COM COCKTAILS
FOR MOVIE NIGHT

Countryman Press

An Imprint of W. W. Norton & Company
Independent Publishers Since 1923

CONTENTS

IT'S ALL ABOUT THE CHEMISTRY

What makes a perfect romantic comedy? And, while we are here, what about the perfect cocktail? Could they have something in common?

The perfect rom-com shouldn't be too sweet or cloying. But we also don't want something too sour or challenging—we are here to enjoy ourselves after all! Perhaps it's about finding the perfect balance, about all the ingredients coming together to create something just a little bit magic.

It's hard to explain why some cocktails have stood the test of time and are still being made and enjoyed a hundred years after they were first concocted, in places like Harry's Bar in Venice (the Bellini), Raffles Hotel's Long Bar in Singapore (the Singapore Sling), or the Manhattan Club in New York (the Manhattan). Maybe we shouldn't try, then—just like we don't need to understand exactly what it is that makes us take Bridget Jones, Sally Albright, or Cher Horowitz into our hearts and cheer them on as they navigate life, love, and relationships. We should just enjoy them.

Sure, some people may claim they don't like rom-coms but, just like cocktails, there's one out there for everyone. Whether you get swept up in the romance of *Sleepless in Seattle*, fall for the classic charms of *Breakfast at Tiffany's,* or laugh out loud at the pratfalls of the *Wedding Crashers*, as the movies themselves show us again and again, you have to be open to possibilities if you are going to find your perfect match.

That is what this book is here to do! In these pages, you will find recipes for 60 cocktails inspired by our favorite rom-coms, designed to bring all their charm straight to your glass. Some you will recognize, some you won't, but you are guaranteed to have a good time while you get to know them. And, remember, sometimes the drink of your dreams might have been there all along, waiting for you to notice it, and other times it might suddenly arrive in your life and change everything. Either way, *Sleepless in Sangria* is here to play matchmaker, making that all-important meet-cute happen.

The traditional romantic-comedy story is all about bringing the couple together—although they have to navigate a few obstacles first, of course. But the movies are about connections for their viewers, too. Is there anything cozier than sitting on the couch with people you care about and putting on a movie you have loved your whole life, or something you have been meaning to see, and laughing (and maybe crying!) together? You could watch with a date, a group of friends, your BFF, or even your parents—introducing them to one of your favorites or watching something they first enjoyed when they were your age. And what better way to celebrate that connection than by making a cocktail to settle down with first?

Whatever you like in a leading lady or leading man— whether you prefer the sass of Reese Witherspoon or the bubbliness of Drew Barrymore; the rugged good looks of Ryan Reynolds or the understated charm of Henry Golding—you will find it all on the screen. No date can be so awkward, no workday so dull, no Sunday afternoon so rainy that a rom-com can't make you feel better.

So, let's raise a glass of whatever cocktail takes your fancy to the magic of rom-coms and make a toast: Here's to finding the cheese to your macaroni.

Most of the cocktails in this book make a single serving, and you can easily multiply the recipes depending on how many you're serving. Glasses are also suggestions, so don't let a lack of specific glassware stop you from having fun! And, if you would be interested in making your own simple syrup, here's an easy guide.

HOW TO MAKE YOUR OWN SIMPLE SYRUP

Essentially, simple syrup is just a mixture of sugar and water and all the recipes in this book require a ratio of 1:1 by volume. However, if you do see the use of 2:1 for other recipes, that simply means doubling the amount of sugar to water. You can make these syrups easily at home and create a batch so you have it on hand whenever you fancy a drink.

A 1:1 mix is possible using a blender: Just add equal amounts of water and sugar to a blender and blend until well mixed. You can also follow the heat method below.

To make a 2:1 syrup, you will generally need heat to ensure the sugar dissolves in the water. Heat the water gently in a pan, add half of the sugar. Stir briefly and leave until the mixture becomes clear. Add the remaining sugar and repeat. Be careful not to over-stir; the mixture will clarify on its own if left without agitation.

THE
RECIPES

I'LL HAVE WHAT SHE'S HAVING

Can rum and lime juice ever be friends? When you add a soupçon of simple syrup, then yes, they can! In fact, these ingredients bring a lightness and bite worthy of a script by the high priestess of rom-coms herself: Nora Ephron. Show your appreciation as loudly as you like.

WHEN HARRY MET DAIQUIRI

INGREDIENTS

1⅔ OZ WHITE RUM	⅔ OZ LIME JUICE	WHEEL OF LIME
	½ OZ SIMPLE SYRUP (SEE PAGE 9)	

Add all the ingredients to a cocktail shaker with a lot of ice. As we know, nothing exciting happens unless you shake things up, so really make sure these ingredients are well combined! Double-strain into a chilled martini glass or champagne coupe. Classically, the daiquiri is garnished with a lime wheel on the rim of the glass, but hey, who said you had to stick to the rules . . .

CLUELESS 1995

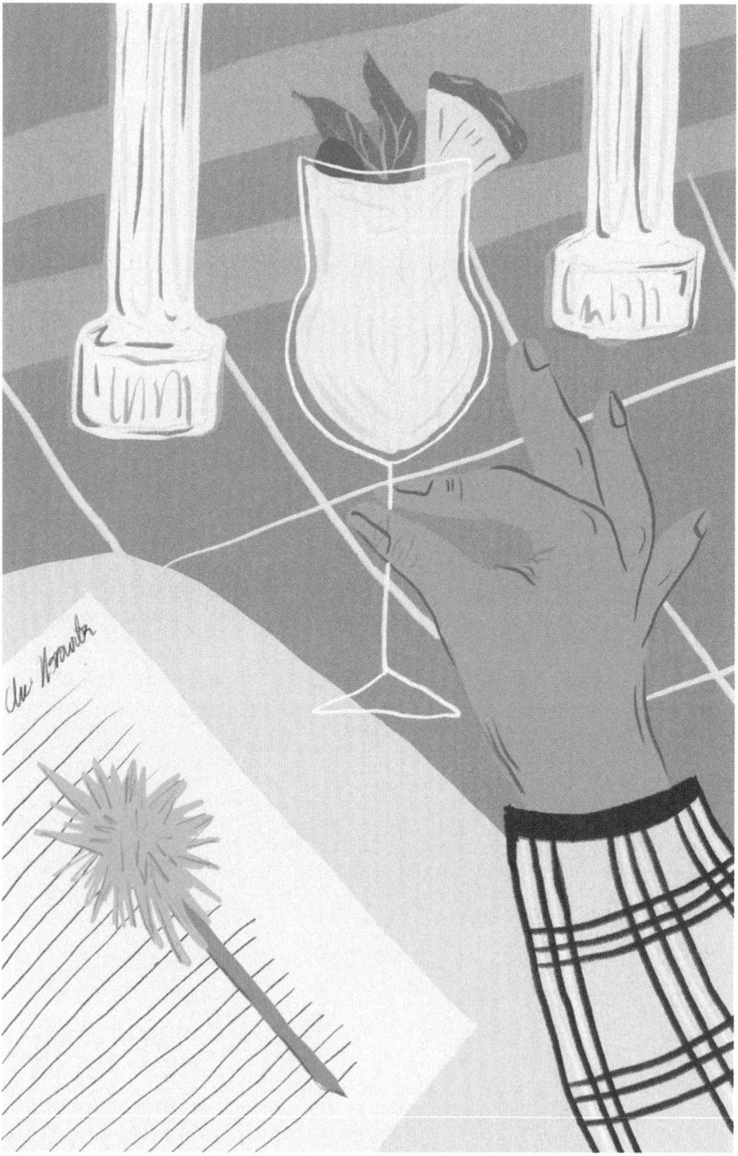

A cocktail that's a little bit extra, but sweet and adorable at the same time, just like everyone's favorite yellow plaid–wearing heroine, Cher Horowitz. Go wild with your garnishes—from pineapple slices and cherries to umbrellas and bright pink straws—to make sure your drink is a total Baldwin, and never a Monet.

CLUELESS COLADA

INGREDIENTS

1⅔ OZ WHITE RUM

1⅔ OZ COCONUT CREAM

5 OZ PINEAPPLE JUICE (OR FRESH PINEAPPLE, BLENDED TO JUICE)

GARNISH OF CHOICE: SLICE OF PINEAPPLE, MARASCHINO CHERRIES, COCKTAIL UMBRELLA . . .

Add all the ingredients to a cocktail shaker with ice and shake well. Strain into a tall glass filled with ice. And don't forget to have fun with those garnishes!

Flavorful botanical gin and zesty lime—they might have competing agendas, but when two ingredients are this evenly matched, sparks are going to fly! Resist it all you want, but no one was ever bored by the perfect Gimlet. Just think carefully before hopping on the back of a strange man's motorcycle while wearing a backless dress.

HOW TO LOSE A GIMLET IN 10 DAYS

INGREDIENTS

1⅔ OZ NAVY-STRENGTH GIN (57% ABV OR HIGHER)	1 OZ LIME JUICE ⅔ OZ SIMPLE SYRUP (SEE PAGE 9)	WHEEL OF LIME

Rose's lime cordial is the old-school option here, but our modern take is brighter and cleaner with fresh lime juice and simple syrup. Add all the ingredients to a cocktail shaker with a lot of ice. Shake well and double-strain into a chilled martini glass or champagne coupe. Garnish with a lime wheel.

This might not be the most elegant of drinks (no one is going to accuse it of having been photoshopped, let's be honest), and it might seem like, well, a bit of a bro. But, just like Jacob Palmer, it has hidden depths. The perfect light and refreshing drink, it deserves to be given a chance.

CRAZY SHANDY LOVE

INGREDIENTS

9 OZ BEER	9 OZ LEMON-LIME SODA	SLICE OF LEMON

Put the lemon slice on the rim of a tall glass or pint glass. Then, while holding your glass at a 45-degree angle, pour in the lemon-lime soda and then the beer. Easy as doing a handstand push-up (if you're Ryan Gosling . . .).

Kat may have had a point that you don't need to do something just because everyone else is doing it, but that doesn't mean you shouldn't give this cocktail a go. Not quite as good as being serenaded by Heath Ledger backed by a full marching band, but close.

10 THINGS I HATE ABOUT WOO WOO

INGREDIENTS

¾ OZ PEACH SCHNAPPS

1⅔ OZ VODKA

4 OZ CRANBERRY JUICE

JUICE OF ¼ LIME

WEDGE OF LIME

Add the peach schnapps, vodka, cranberry juice, and lime juice to a cocktail shaker filled with ice. Shake and strain into a tall tumbler half-filled with ice. Garnish with a lime wedge.

Maybe there is a bossy ghost in your apartment, maybe you just have an annoying housemate. Either way, forget work for a while and try this punchy cocktail that was originally designed to wake the dead—or, well, quite the hungover. It's what Reese Witherspoon would have wanted.

The Tenant Reviver

INGREDIENTS

¾ OZ GIN	¾ OZ LILLET BLANC VERMOUTH	2–3 DASHES ABSINTHE
¾ OZ TRIPLE SEC	¾ OZ LEMON JUICE	TWIST OF LEMON

Add all the ingredients to a cocktail shaker with ice and shake well. Strain into a large balloon glass or champagne coupe. Garnish with a lemon twist.

If you've never tried this boozy, champagne-fueled cocktail, then it's time to lose your V-card. And if people talk—well, let them. Rom-com heroes and heroines don't listen to gossip and that's why they get to ride off into the sunset with the person of their choosing at the end. In this case, on a lawnmower.

EASY (A)MBROSIA

INGREDIENTS

¾ OZ COGNAC	1 TSP TRIPLE SEC	CHAMPAGNE
¾ OZ CALVADOS	1 TSP LEMON JUICE	TWIST OF LEMON

Pour all the ingredients (except for the champagne) into a cocktail shaker. Add ice and shake well. Strain into a champagne flute or coupe, top up with champagne exactly to your liking, garnish with a lemon twist, and serve immediately.

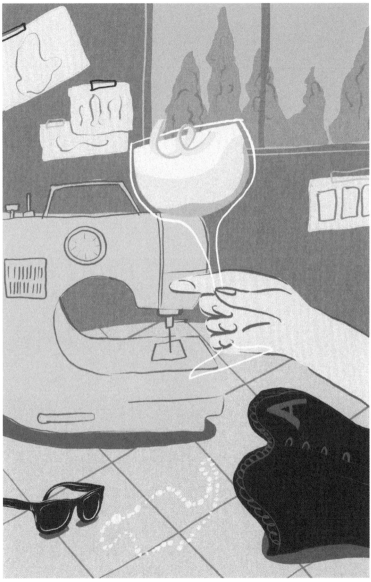

What? You might be thinking, *Whiskey, absinthe, egg white, lemon, AND lime?* Well, sometimes you just can't predict who or what you are going to be attracted to. It might be essentially a grown-up Southern Comfort and 7-Up, it might be a chauvinistic Gerard Butler. Just try to avoid a super-awkward kiss in an elevator.

MORNING SHOW FIZZ

INGREDIENTS

1⅔ OZ SCOTCH WHISKEY

¾ OZ LEMON AND LIME JUICE (50:50 MIX)

½ OZ SIMPLE SYRUP (SEE PAGE 9)

1 EGG WHITE

1–2 DASHES ABSINTHE

CLUB SODA

SLICE OF ORANGE

Add all the ingredients (except the club soda) to a cocktail shaker. Shake without ice to emulsify the egg white. Add ice and shake again. Strain into a tall tumbler (no ice) and top up with club soda. Finish with an orange slice.

Warning: This cocktail packs a punch, so go easy—particularly in times of emotional turmoil, like if you find out your dad is dating your ex. Drink too many of these and the ending will be somewhat predictable. . . . It's a good drink though, so try it once, and if you want to commit, well, that's up to you!

No Strings Between the Sheets

INGREDIENTS

⅔ OZ WHITE RUM	⅔ OZ COINTREAU	TWIST OF LIME
⅔ OZ COGNAC	⅓ OZ LEMON JUICE	

Add all the ingredients to a cocktail shaker filled with ice and shake well. Strain into a chilled balloon glass or champagne coupe. Garnish with a lime twist.

What would you do differently knowing what you know now? That's a pretty profound question and, realistically, one probably best tackled after a cocktail. We all dreamed of being popular and grown-up when we were 13, but adulthood isn't all Manhattan apartments and cool jobs working for magazines. Never mind, though—good friends, cocktails, and rom-coms is a pretty good deal, even without access to magic dust.

Matty-dor

INGREDIENTS

1 OZ BLANCO TEQUILA

⅔ OZ LIME JUICE

2 OZ PINEAPPLE JUICE

SLICE OF FRUIT

Add all the ingredients to a cocktail shaker. Shake hard over ice to ensure that the pineapple juice is well mixed (until it becomes a smooth texture and a foam develops on top). Strain into a chilled balloon glass or champagne coupe. Garnish with a slice of fruit, like a lime slice or pineapple wedge.

Ah! A pre-McConaissance rom-com classic, from back in the days when he was happy to play charming bad boys with a good heart. Don't get stuck drinking the same thing because it's comfortable and easy—instead, try this zippy cocktail with a kick. Just like SJP and McConaughey, lime and tequila really do have the perfect chemistry.

Tripp Sour

INGREDIENTS

1⅔ OZ TEQUILA

¾ OZ LIME JUICE

⅔ OZ SIMPLE SYRUP (SEE PAGE 9)

1 EGG WHITE OR 1 OZ WHIPPED AQUAFABA

SLICE OF APPLE

MARASCHINO CHERRIES

Add all the ingredients to a cocktail shaker. Shake first without ice to emulsify the egg. Then add ice and shake again. Strain into a short tumbler or rocks glass over ice. Garnish with an apple slice and a cherry or two.

Underestimate this cocktail at your peril. Sure, it might look kind of pink and frivolous but, as Elle Woods is here to teach us, appearances can be deceiving: this is actually a classic Cuban cocktail that goes back to the Prohibition era. You could make a strong case that it is even better than spending four hours in a hot tub after winter formal.

ELLE SORORITY PRESIDENTE

INGREDIENTS

2 OZ RUM	⅓ OZ CURAÇAO OR TRIPLE SEC	WEDGE OF ORANGE
1 OZ DRY VERMOUTH	1 DASH GRENADINE	

Fill a mixing glass with ice. Add all the ingredients and stir until chilled. Strain into a chilled martini glass or short tumbler and garnish with an orange wedge. Then the prosecution may rest.

Whether you loved high school, like Rob, or it was a traumatic time of not quite fitting in, like Josie, let it all go and make yourself this classic cocktail, while wondering if South Glen High should maybe have had some security measures in place to stop adult reporters from spying on their students . . .

JOSIE'S JULEP

INGREDIENTS

A COUPLE SPRIGS OF MINT, PLUS MORE FOR GARNISH	2 OZ BOURBON	$\frac{2}{3}$ OZ SIMPLE SYRUP (SEE PAGE 9)

Add all of the ingredients to a short tumbler or julep cup and stir gently. Leave for 10 minutes or so for the mint to infuse. Add crushed ice and churn with a spoon (preferably a bar spoon as the metal disc on one end is perfect for pulling the mint up through the ice). Top up with more ice and churn again. Garnish with an additional mint sprig or two. If you want to be super-profesh, slap the mint against your hand a couple of times first to bring out the mint oils.

SUMMER OF LOVE

A drink that you just won't be able to stop thinking about, and one that's perfect for a beach holiday—whether or not you run into your ex there. As the wisdom of Kunu might have it, if life hands you limes, at least you've got one of the ingredients for a great Mai Tai.

FORGETTING SARAH MAI TAI

INGREDIENTS

1 OZ JAMAICAN RUM

1 OZ AGRICOLE RUM

1 OZ LIME JUICE

½ OZ CURAÇAO

⅓ OZ ORGEAT SYRUP

⅓ OZ SIMPLE SYRUP (SEE PAGE 9)

GARNISH OF CHOICE: CHUNK OF PINEAPPLE, SPRIG OF MINT, MARASCHINO CHERRIES, COCKTAIL UMBRELLA . . .

Add all the ingredients to a cocktail shaker filled with some crushed or cracked ice and shake well. Strain into a short tumbler filled with ice and garnish with a pineapple chunk, cherries, a mint spring, and an umbrella if you have one on hand.

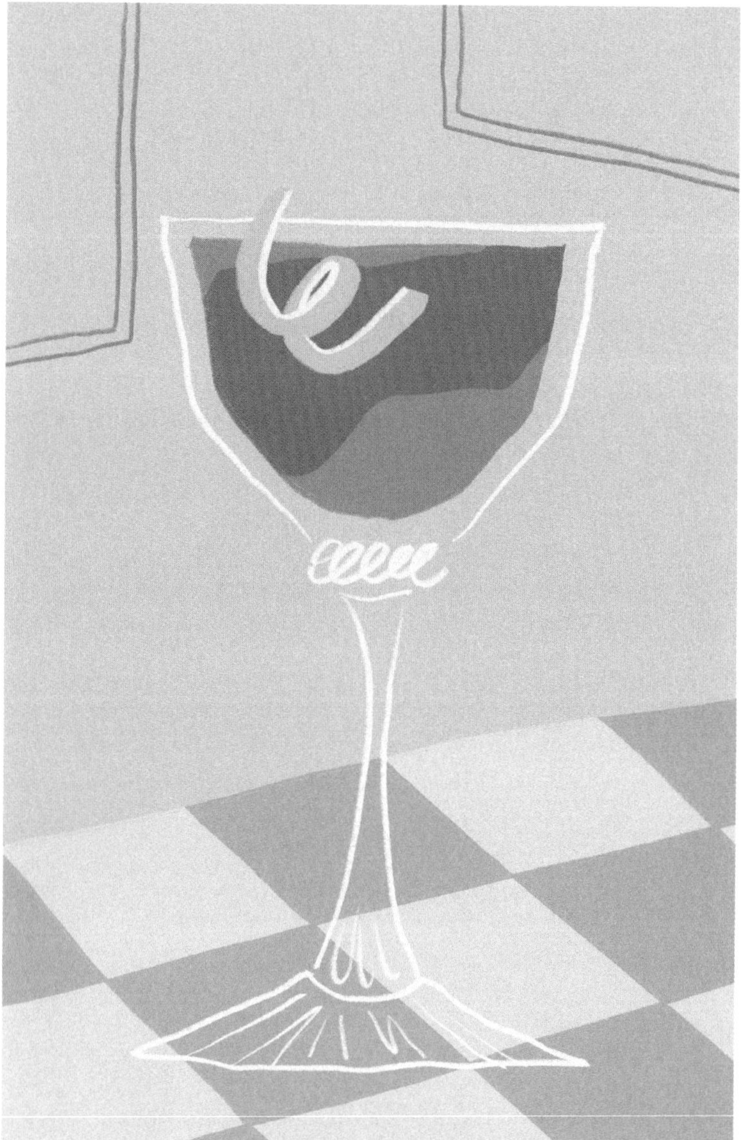

Before Tom met Meg, there was Daryl Hannah: a beautiful mermaid with hair we were all obsessed with when we were seven. A sweeter, lighter version of a Martini, this is a perfect New York drink that Madison would surely approve of. You can drink it in the bath if you like, but in that case, maybe just limit it to one!

TOM HANKY PANKY

INGREDIENTS

1½ OZ SWEET VERMOUTH
1½ OZ GIN

2 DASHES FERNET-BRANCA

TWIST OF ORANGE

Put all the ingredients into a mixing glass filled with ice. Stir and strain into a martini glass or champagne coupe—chilled if possible, you want this drink colder than the Hudson River—and garnish with a neatly twirled orange twist.

TOP 3
TOM HANK
ROM-COMS

1
SLEEPLESS IN SEATTLE
(1993)

2
YOU'VE GOT MAIL
(1998)

3
SPLASH
(1984)

Whether your life is currently one big musical number or your boss has decided you are only fit to write condolence cards, a chilled and herby Mojito could be just what you need. It's a perfect drink if you are tired of sweet, fruity cocktails and you're looking for a different perspective.

500 FLAVORS OF MOJITO

INGREDIENTS

⅔ OZ LIME JUICE

½ OZ SIMPLE SYRUP (SEE PAGE 9)

A COUPLE SPRIGS OF MINT, PLUS MORE FOR GARNISH

1⅔ OZ WHITE RUM

CLUB SODA

Add the lime juice, simple syrup, and mint leaves to a tall tumbler. Lightly muddle the mixture. Add the rum and fill the glass halfway with ice. Stir well with a bar spoon and top with more ice to fill the glass, then add a splash of club soda to taste. Garnish with additional mint sprigs. The amount of ice in this drink makes it much easier to drink with a straw! Sip thoughtfully while contemplating architecture.

Much like Melanie Smooter/Carmichael, this is a cocktail that seems to be made up of parts that don't quite fit together—American whiskey and the English classic sloe gin? Whaaaat? But shake it all up and somehow it works. Sure, other drinks might have the refinement of a proposal in Tiffany's, but where's the fun in that?

SWEET HOME ALABAMA SLAMMER

INGREDIENTS

¾ OZ AMERICAN WHISKEY OR BOURBON

¾ OZ SLOE GIN

¾ OZ AMARETTO

1⅔ OZ ORANGE JUICE (FRESHLY SQUEEZED IS BEST)

WEDGE OF ORANGE

MARASCHINO CHERRY

Add all the spirits and the orange juice to a cocktail shaker filled with ice. Shake well and strain into a small tumbler or martini glass over ice. Garnish with an orange wedge and cherry.

It's the classic drink that everyone wants. But there's no need to fight over it, and you won't have to hire a private investigator to find it, as the recipe is right here! It's perfect for a lazy late brunch or a Sunday pick-me-up and, while no one is about to claim that cocktails are good for you, a good dose of tomato juice is certainly a heartening addition.

There's Something About (Bloody) Mary

INGREDIENTS

1⅔ OZ VODKA

3⅓ OZ TOMATO JUICE

TABASCO SAUCE (4–10 DROPS, DEPENDING ON HOW HOT YOU WANT THINGS TO GET)

WORCESTERSHIRE SAUCE (2–5 DROPS)

A SPLASH OF LEMON JUICE

BLACK PEPPER (1–2 TWISTS OF A PEPPER GRINDER)

A PINCH OF SALT (CELERY SALT WORKS WELL IF YOU HAVE IT)

GARNISH OF CHOICE: CELERY, OLIVES, LLEMON, PICKLES . . .

Add all the ingredients to a cocktail shaker, but be careful with the Tabasco and Worcestershire sauces, so you get the kick just how you like it. You might want to play around with the quantity of lemon juice, too. Add ice and roll the cocktail shaker, turning it over slowly to allow the ingredients to mix and chill—don't go nuts and shake it as you'll make the drink too watery. Strain into a chilled highball glass, with or without ice. A celery stick is the classic garnish, but you can be more inventive or over-the-top if you like!

It's not clear why only boys get to travel through time, but in rom-com cocktail land, everyone can change their future—for one, by learning to make this classic rum cocktail! It's definitely something you'll want to revisit, and it serves as a perfect accompaniment to a game of ping-pong with Bill Nighy.

BACK IN TIME

INGREDIENTS

⅓ OZ SIMPLE SYRUP (SEE PAGE 9)   2–3 DASHES ANGOSTURA BITTERS   COIN OF ORANGE PEEL

1⅔ OZ GOLDEN OR DARK RUM

Add a large orange peel coin to the bottom of a rocks glass along with the simple syrup, bitters, and ¾ ounces of the rum. Add two cubes of ice and stir for 20 to 30 seconds to dilute. Add the remaining rum, two more ice cubes, and stir again.

What's not to love about this cocktail? It's fun, it's silly, it's sweet, and it couldn't be easier. Whether you are in Greece trying to untangle some potentially complicated family dynamics, or at home on the couch on a rainy Saturday, let's sing it together: Cuba Libre—how can we resist you?!

MAMMA CUBA LIBRE

INGREDIENTS

| 2–3 LIME WEDGES | 1⅔ OZ RUM | 2⅓–3⅓ OZ COLA |

Fill a tumbler with ice. Squeeze in the lime wedges, add the rum, and top up with cola. Add more ice to fill the glass (more ice means it won't melt so fast and dilute your drink) or more cola if you need to, but be careful not to overdilute the rum.

Wouldn't it be nice to drive out to the Hawaiian countryside to pick a fresh pineapple? (Without the amnesia-causing accident, obviously.) If that's not an option where you live, you can make every day special by trying this boozy-but-delightfully-tropical cocktail, and settling down to watch the rom-com with more meet-cutes than any other.

OOPSY [BRANDY] DAISY

INGREDIENTS

1⅔ OZ COGNAC

⅓ OZ TRIPLE SEC OR CURAÇAO

⅔ OZ LEMON JUICE

1 TSP SIMPLE SYRUP (SEE PAGE 9)

CLUB SODA

2 DASHES JAMAICAN RUM

SPRIG OF MINT

FRUIT OF YOUR CHOICE: FRESH PINEAPPLE, BLACKBERRIES, MARASCHINO CHERRIES . . .

Add the cognac, triple sec or curaçao, lemon juice, and simple syrup to a cocktail shaker filled with with ice. Shake well and strain into a large wine glass or julep cup filled with ice. Add a splash of club soda and finish with a couple of dashes of Jamaican rum over the top. Garnish with fruit—blackberries and cherries look good if you don't go for the pineapple—and a sprig of mint for freshness. Watch out for penguins on the road!

Maybe they'll call you, maybe they won't. Maybe they like you, maybe they don't. If they're not putting the effort in, then they're not the one for you. They're no Bradley Cooper or Jennifer Aniston anyway. This fun, flirty cocktail is the perfect solution to any uninspiring date.

HE'S JUST NOT THAT INTO SEX ON THE BEACH

INGREDIENTS

1⅔ OZ VODKA

¾ OZ PEACH SCHNAPPS

¾ OZ CRÈME DE CASSIS (OPTIONAL)

2 OZ CRANBERRY JUICE

2 OZ FRESHLY SQUEEZED ORANGE JUICE

WEDGE OF ORANGE

MARASCHINO CHERRY

Pour the vodka, peach schnapps, and crème de cassis (for a little extra fruitiness, if you fancy it) into a highball glass two-thirds filled with ice. Add the cranberry juice and stir to combine. Slowly pour the freshly squeezed orange juice on top. Garnish with an orange wedge and cherry.

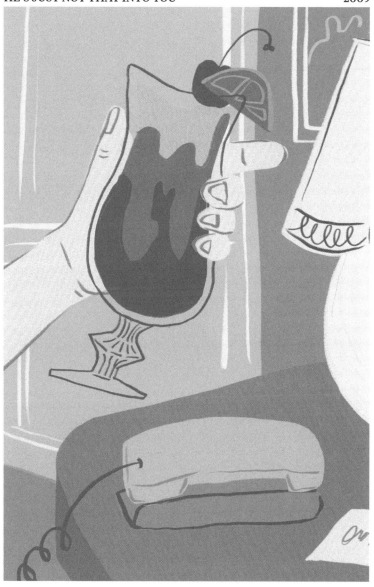

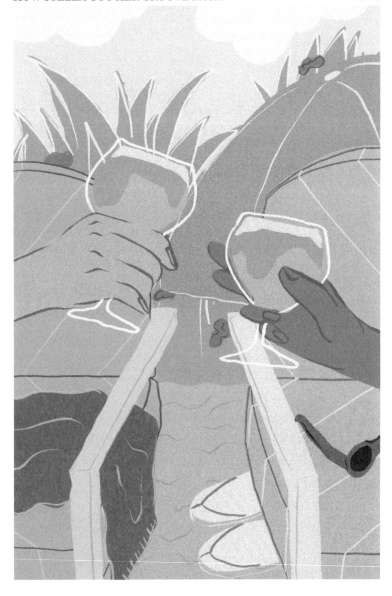

In a decade when rom-coms tended to feature blonde women dating older men, we needed Stella Payne to women shake things up—even more than she needed that holiday in Jamaica. So whip up this punch and pretend you're in an island paradise, about to meet your very own sexy chef.

STELLA'S GINGER BREW

INGREDIENTS

1⅓ OZ GIN	1⅔ OZ LEMON JUICE	1 SMALL BOTTLE OF BEER
	1⅔ OZ GINGER SYRUP	

Add the gin, lemon juice, and ginger syrup to a blender with a couple of ice cubes. Blend. Fine-strain the mixture into a chilled balloon glass. Top up with beer.

Were eggs from Juli Baker's chickens ever used to make a Rum Flip?
It feels unlikely, but don't let that stop you, as this old-school cocktail
comes with a heavy dose of nostalgia—just like the movie itself.
Even if it doesn't seem that appealing to begin with, you'll fall for its
charms in the end.

RUM FLIPPED

INGREDIENTS

1⅔ OZ RUM	¾ OZ SIMPLE SYRUP (SEE PAGE 9)	WHOLE NUTMEG
	1 EGG	

Add the rum and simple syrup to a cocktail shaker. Crack the egg
directly into the shaker. Shake without ice to emulsify the egg, then
add ice and shake again. Strain into a chilled large wine glass or champagne coupe and garnish with
freshly grated nutmeg.

When Princess Ann, played by Audrey Hepburn, becomes burnt out by too many royal duties, her doctor recommends that she take a break and do whatever she wants for a while. Who can argue with that? This classic American drink is guaranteed to sweep you up in the romance of Hollywood—even if it can't promise Gregory Peck will turn up on his Vespa.

Ro-Manhattan Holiday

INGREDIENTS

2 OZ AMERICAN WHISKEY, BOURBON, OR RYE

⅔ OZ VERMOUTH (DRY, SWEET, OR A 50:50 MIXTURE OF BOTH, DEPENDING ON HOW YOU LIKE IT!)

2–3 DASHES BITTERS

MARASCHINO CHERRY OR TWIST OF LEMON (OPTIONAL)

Fill a mixing glass with ice. Add all of the ingredients and stir until chilled. Strain into a chilled glass. This drink works by itself, but if you'd like, you can garnish with a cherry if you prefer it sweet or perfect, or a lemon twist for those who want it dry.

DOWN-
TOWN
DRINKS

No promises, but a chance encounter with this drink might just change your life. Whether you live in Notting Hill or Beverly Hills, or somewhere completely different, this is a cocktail that brings people together. Just be careful that after a few of these, you don't decide to climb into any private gardens. Whoopsidaisies.

NOTTING BELLINI

INGREDIENTS

ONE 750 ML BOTTLE PROSECCO   4 RIPE WHITE PEACHES

Peel and pit your peaches and blend the fruit in a food processor or with an immersion blender until smooth. Refrigerate your peach purée for at least 20 minutes (or until chilled). Either in a jug or in individual champagne flutes, combine one part peach purée with two parts prosecco. Stir to combine.

ROM-COM KINGS

HOLLYWOOD'S HIGHEST-GROSSING ROM-COM ACTORS

1
HUGH GRANT

2
RICHARD GERE

3
BEN STILLER

(SOURCE: THE NUMBERS)

"Kiki! Kiki! Make me an Americano Sweetheart!" Whether you have your own personal assistant to rustle up your cocktails for you or not, this drink is worth trying. It may not be as famous as its boozy big sister, the Negroni, but it has an understated charm that shouldn't be overlooked. That cocktail you saw by the pool? It was this one!

Americano Sweethearts

INGREDIENTS

1²⁄₃ OZ CAMPARI	1²⁄₃ OZ SWEET VERMOUTH	WEDGE OF ORANGE
	CLUB SODA	

Fill a tall glass with ice. Add the Campari and sweet vermouth. Top with club soda to your taste, stir to mix, and garnish an orange wedge.

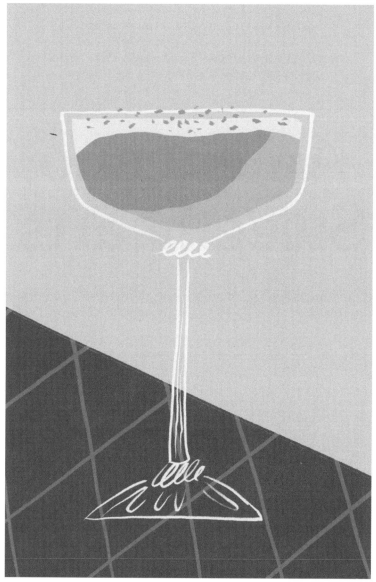

Jennifer Aniston's Kate Mosley clearly did not get the memo from *The Wedding Date's* Kat about what inevitably happens when you pay a guy to pretend to be your fiancé. But we can forgive that (though we may raise an eyebrow at a boss who sees an engagement as a prerequisite for promoting someone) as this movie, just like this cocktail, has a certain sweet, old-fashioned charm that is hard to resist.

BOSTON BOUND

INGREDIENTS

1⅔ OZ BOURBON	⅓ OZ SYRUP (SEE PAGE 9)	WHOLE NUTMEG
1⅔ OZ MADEIRA	1 EGG	

Add the bourbon, Madeira, and simple syrup to a cocktail shaker, then crack in the egg. Shake without ice to emulsify the egg, then add ice and shake again. Strain into a chilled martini glass or champagne coupe and garnish with a light sprinkle of freshly grated nutmeg.

Maybe you tried to make this cocktail before and it didn't go so well. Perhaps you ended up with a murky pink mess rather than the sunrise of your dreams. But now you have this recipe, would you do it all over again? Of course you would! See you in Montauk.

Eternal Tequila Sunrise of the Spotless Mind

INGREDIENTS

1⅔ OZ TEQUILA	2½ OZ ORANGE JUICE	WEDGE OF ORANGE
	½ OZ GRENADINE	

Add the tequila and orange juice to a cocktail shaker. Fill with ice and shake. Strain into a tall tumbler glass filled with ice. Gently pour the grenadine down the side of the glass; it is a dense, sticky syrup and will sink to the bottom, creating the sunrise effect. Garnish with an orange wedge.

Put on your chicest black dress and largest sunglasses and whip up this homage to the bee's knees of all romantic movies. It's the perfect drink for many occasions, from a swinging party in a New York apartment to suddenly feeling the urge to sing something wistful on a fire escape.

Bee's Knees at Tiffany's

INGREDIENTS

| 2 OZ GIN | ⅔ OZ LEMON JUICE | ⅔ OZ HONEY SYRUP (3 PARTS HONEY TO 1 PART WATER) |

Add the ingredients into an ice-filled cocktail shaker. Shake and strain into a chilled coupe. Evening gloves optional.

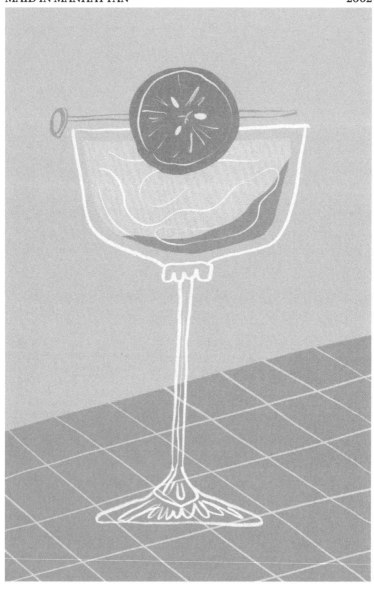

If the glamour of downtown Manhattan seems a world away, this movie *and* this cocktail may be just what you need to remind you that all it takes is a fancy coat and some J.Lo-level sass to change your life. If you're paying attention, you'll realize this is actually a "maid"-style cocktail and not a Manhattan. Plot twist!

Maid's Manhattan

INGREDIENTS

1 DASH ABSINTHE	A SPRIG OF MINT	2 OZ WHITE RUM
4 SLICES CUCUMBER	½ OZ SIMPLE SYRUP (SEE PAGE 9)	1⅔ OZ CLUB SODA SODA WATER
	1 OZ LIME JUICE	

Add the dash of absinthe to an ice-filled cocktail glass. Top with cold tap water and leave to stand. Put three of the cucumber slices, mint, simple syrup, and lime juice into a shaker and stir gently to bruise the mint. Then add rum and ice and shake. Empty the cocktail glass and then double-strain the shaker into the cocktail glass. Top up with club soda to taste, and garnish with the last slice of cucumber.

We've all been tempted to put that shiny, lovely new thing on the credit card, but as Rebecca Bloomwood is here to show us, the pursuit of material goods can only get us so far. So, instead of logging onto Shein, why not don your best green scarf, mix up this cocktail, and enjoy some vicarious shopping with Isla Fisher instead.

DITSY BRITZY SPRITZ

INGREDIENTS

1¼ OZ KAMM & SONS	1⅔ OZ SPARKLING WHITE WINE	2 WEDGES OF GRAPEFRUIT
½ OZ ELDERFLOWER CORDIAL	1⅔ OZ CLUB SODA SODA WATER	

Pour all the ingredients into a glass filled with ice and stir well.
Squeeze one wedge of grapefruit into the cocktail and
garnish with the fresh wedge of grapefruit.

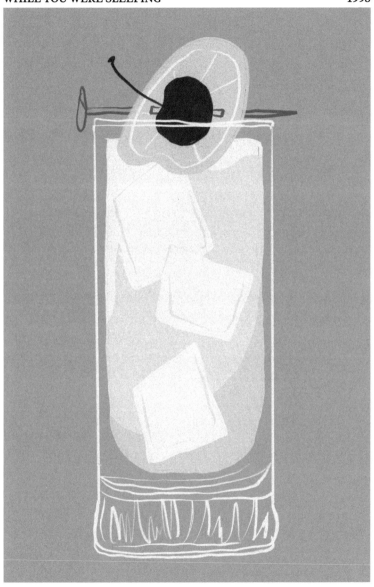

While probably not many of us have been in a situation where we have saved someone's life and then fallen for their brother, it can be all-too-easy to get unexpectedly entangled in a misunderstanding and not know how to get out of it. So, let's keep things simple here, at least, with this sweet-and-sour gin tipple. Don't stay in the booth, Lucy!

Chicago Collins

INGREDIENTS

1²⁄₃ OZ GIN	²⁄₃ OZ SIMPLE SYRUP (SEE PAGE 9)	WEDGE OF LEMON
¾ OZ LEMON JUICE	CLUB SODA	MARASCHINO CHERRY

Fill a tall tumbler glass with ice. Add the gin, lemon juice, and simple syrup. Top with club soda, add more ice, if necessary, to fill the glass, and stir to mix. Garnish with a lemon wedge and a cherry.

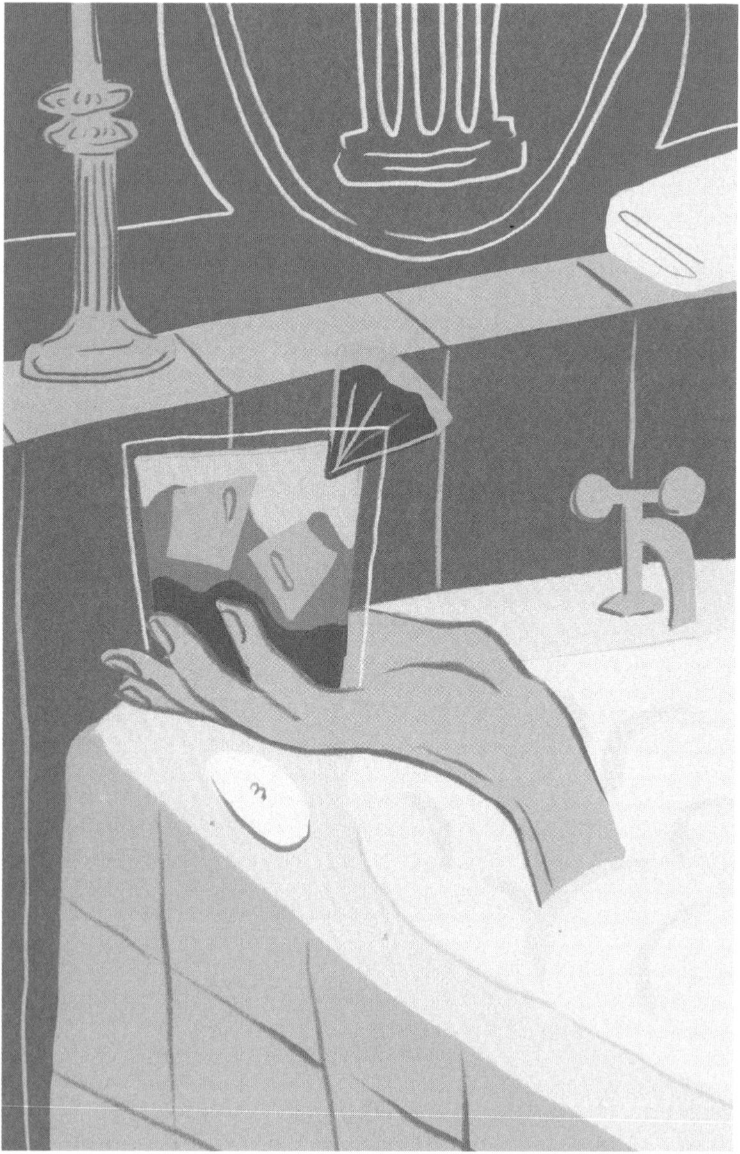

If you've never had a Paloma before, imagine a margarita got all dressed up to take a private jet to the opera. It's better than a shopping trip on Rodeo Drive and could even cheer up a sad millionaire. In fact, it's so good, you might pee your pants.

PALOMA WOMAN

INGREDIENTS

WEDGE OF LIME	2 OZ TEQUILA	2 OZ PINK GRAPEFRUIT JUICE
FINE SEA SALT	$2/3$ OZ LIME JUICE	WEDGE OF GRAPEFRUIT
	$1/3$ OZ AGAVE SYRUP	

Put a tablespoon or so of fine sea salt on a plate. Rub a lime wedge around the edge of a highball glass, turn it upside-down, and press it into the plate, coating the rim of the glass with the salt. Put the tequila, lime juice, agave syrup, and pink grapefruit juice in a cocktail shaker. Add ice, shake, and strain into the glass filled with ice, if you like your drinks as cool as Vivian's thigh-high boots. Garnish with a grapefruit wedge.

In one version of this story, you don't try this cocktail. You carry on as you were before, missing all the signs that are right in front of you, and your life stays the way it was. But is that the version of the story you want? No. So grab your cocktail shaker and put on the movie that showed us what a break-up haircut is supposed to look like.

SLIDING SLING

INGREDIENTS

1 OZ GIN
1/3 OZ COINTREAU
1/3 OZ BENEDICTINE
½ OZ HEERING CHERRY LIQUEUR

½ OZ LIME JUICE
1/3 OZ GRENADINE
1 DASH ANGOSTURA BITTERS
4 OZ PINEAPPLE JUICE

FRUIT SLICE OF CHOICE: ORANGE, LEMON, PINEAPPLE . . .
MARASCHINO CHERRY OR RASPBERRY

Add all the ingredients to a cocktail shaker with ice. Shake and strain into a tall tumbler filled with ice. Serve with a fruit slice (orange, lemon, and pineapple all work well) and something like a cherry or raspberry.

Whether it's Paris Fashion Week or just a regular Friday night, you'll want to put together your most stylish outfit for this one. It's the perfect drink with which to impress the boss—or anyone really. This cocktail is even cooler than Meryl Streep's icy stare.

EL DESIGNER DIABLO

INGREDIENTS

1⅔ OZ TEQUILA	¾ OZ LIME JUICE	GINGER ALE
¾ OZ CRÈME DE CASSIS		WEDGE OF LIME

Add the tequila, créme de cassis, and lime juice to a tall tumbler glass filled with ice and mix. Top with ginger ale and garnish with a lime wedge.

You might not have guessed it, but rum, brandy, and citrus make for the perfect cocktail mixtape. If you've been jumping from drink to drink and struggling to commit, then take this opportunity to put on a record and find out if this is the cocktail you have been waiting for . . .

HIGH(BALL) FIDELITY

INGREDIENTS

1²⁄₃ OZ WHITE RUM	1²⁄₃ OZ ORANGE JUICE	²⁄₃ OZ ORGEAT SYRUP
²⁄₃ OZ BRANDY OR COGNAC	1 OZ LEMON JUICE	SLICE OF ORANGE

Add all the ingredients to a cocktail shaker filled with ice, shake well, and strain into an ice-filled highball glass. Garnish with a slice of orange. If you have some music-loving friends coming over, this also works well as a punch, ideally served from a suitably vintage punch bowl. Scale up the ingredients accordingly, and, if you can, chill with a big single ice cube to avoid diluting the drink too much (fill a suitable container with water and freeze overnight).

Sure, there's a whole world of glitzy, complicated cocktails out there and there's nothing stopping you from trying every one. But what if the right cocktail for you is something simpler, something that's maybe been there all along? When you're ready to come home to a good, honest drink that truly understands you, you'll know where to find this Martini. Just don't eat the napkin.

ALWAYS BE MY MARTINI

INGREDIENTS

½ OZ DRY VERMOUTH	2 OZ GIN	OLIVES

Fill a mixing glass (ideally one that's been in the fridge, as you want this drink as cold as possible) with ice, add the vermouth, and stir to coat the ice. If you like your martini dry, strain out some of the vermouth and discard it. Add the gin and stir until chilled and diluted—this takes the edge off the neat gin. Strain into a chilled martini glass and garnish with olives.

TIPPLES
TO SAY
I DO TO

Talking of doing the same things over and over, why does Katherine Heigl keep falling for cynical men who don't believe in marriage? Whether you love being a bridesmaid, or would rather shirk the responsibility and get seated at the "naughty table" with all the other people the bride and groom don't trust to behave, this is the perfect drink to round off a day of celebrating someone else's (hopefully) happy-ever-after.

Choose Me Negroni

INGREDIENTS

1 OZ GIN

1 OZ CAMPARI
1 OZ SWEET VERMOUTH

SLICE OR TWIST OF ORANGE

Add all the alcohol to an ice-filled rocks glass and stir (one or two large ice cubes are much better than a load of small ones here). Garnish with an orange slice or twist.

Just because everyone else is doing it, doesn't mean you have to as well. Take your time, and only have an alcoholic drink when you want one, not because you are being pressured into it. If you listen to other people, you'll end up with all the wrong cocktails. There's no shame in going virgin.

THE 40-YEAR-OLD VIRGIN MARGARITA

INGREDIENTS

WEDGE OF LIME	1²/₃ OZ NONALCOHOLIC TEQUILA	1 OZ ORANGE JUICE
FINE SEA SALT	1 OZ LIME JUICE	WHEEL OF LIME

To salt the rim of the margarita glass, run a wedge of lime around it, and then touch it to a plate covered with fine sea salt. Add all the ingredients to a shaker with ice, shake well, and carefully strain into the glass. Garnish with a lime wheel.

It's a truth universally acknowledged in the rom-com world that weddings can make us do crazy things. Sure, maybe you've never hired an escort in a mistaken attempt to save face, but there's bound to have been something crazy and, whatever it was, hopefully you had your very own TJ—the queen of all movie best friends—to bail you out.

NICK'S MARTINI

INGREDIENTS

2 OZ NAVY-STRENGTH GIN	$^2/_3$ OZ DRY VERMOUTH	WEDGE OR TWIST OF CITRUS OF YOUR CHOICE

Add the ingredients to a mixing glass filled with ice. Stir until well chilled and diluted. Strain into a martini glass or champagne coupe. Garnish with a citrus wedge or twist—whichever you think best matches your style of gin.

Being unexpectedly serenaded on a crowded airplane may not be for everyone, but this cocktail is a guaranteed crowd-pleaser. Whether you're planning a wedding or a fun night in curled up with a rom-com, pop the prosecco and pour yourself a drink that's as heartwarming as Julia and Robbie themselves. (Van Halen T-shirt optional.)

THE WEDDING SPRITZ

INGREDIENTS

2½ OZ PROSECCO	¾ OZ CLUB SODA	SLICES OF ORANGE
1⅔ OZ APEROL		

Add all the ingredients into a large wine glass filled with ice.
Gently stir and garnish with orange slices.

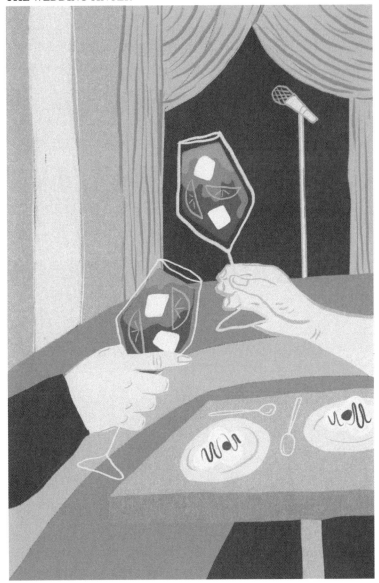

ROM-COM QUEENS

HOLLYWOOD'S HIGHEST-GROSSING ROM-COM ACTRESSES

1

JULIA ROBERTS

2

JENNIFER ANISTON

3

DREW BARRYMORE

Everyone wants the perfect wedding, but as Kate
Hudson and Anne Hathaway are here to show us, there's
really no need to rugby tackle your best friend to the floor as she
walks down the aisle. Instead, take the heat out of the preparations
for the big day with a lovely, chilled, rom-com cocktail.

A Cosmopolitan Feud

INGREDIENTS

1 OZ VODKA	½ OZ LIME JUICE	TWIST OF ORANGE
½ OZ TRIPLE SEC	1 OZ CRANBERRY JUICE	

Put all the ingredients into a cocktail shaker filled with ice. Shake well and strain into a chilled martini glass. Garnish with an orange twist.

I do solemnly declare that I know of no lawful impediment why raspberry and Chambord should not be joined together with vodka, in this fun and flirty take on a Martini. Whether you're off to a posh wedding or not, you won't want to miss a great opportunity to try it. Note: It may taste better if drunk while wearing a giant early nineties hat.

Four Weddings and a French Martini

INGREDIENTS

1²/₃ OZ VODKA	1²/₃ OZ PINEAPPLE JUICE	RASPBERRY
½ OZ CHAMBORD LIQUEUR		

Add the vodka, Chambord, and pineapple juice to a cocktail shaker filled with ice. Shake and strain into a chilled martini glass. Garnish with a raspberry, and drink while putting on your best posh English accent.

Put whoever you want on a pedestal, but make you
sure you put this drink in your hand! As George would probably
say, there might not be a wedding to go to, there might not even be
dancing, but by god, this is a great cocktail to help you celebrate
any moment you choose!

A Champagne Toast

INGREDIENTS

¾ OZ VODKA	½ OZ ELDERFLOWER LIQUEUR OR CORDIAL	CHAMPAGNE (AROUND 2½ OZ)

Add the vodka and elderflower liqueur to a cocktail shaker filled with ice. Shake well and strain into a
champagne flute or coupe and top with Champagne.

It's hard to get it right if you don't know what you truly want, as Julia Roberts is here to teach us. Which is great advice, but less of an issue with this cocktail, which is so easy you won't need a dress rehearsal. Like the movie, the Bramble is a modern invention with something of the enduring classic about it—and it might just get to you too . . .

BRIDE'S BRAMBLE

INGREDIENTS

2 OZ GIN	½ OZ SIMPLE SYRUP (SEE PAGE 9)	BLACKBERRIES
1 OZ LEMON JUICE	½ OZ CRÈME DE MÛRE LIQUEUR	

Shake the gin, lemon juice, and simple syrup together in a cocktail shaker filled with ice. Strain into a short tumbler filled with ice. Stir. Gently add more ice cubes to fill the glass. Trickle the crème de mûre over the top and garnish with fresh blackberries.

This high-octane cocktail may appear, at first glance, to be nothing more than a regular suburban pink Martini, but it's simply playing a part. The concealed weapon here—rather than a career as an assassin carefully hidden from your spouse—is a single shot of absinthe. Underestimate it at your peril.

CONCEALED WEAPONS

INGREDIENTS

¾ OZ ABSINTHE

¾ OZ CHAMBORD LIQUEUR

⅔ OZ LEMON JUICE

½ OZ SIMPLE SYRUP (SEE PAGE 9)

1 DASH ANGOSTURA BITTERS

1 DASH PEYCHAUD'S BITTERS

½ EGG WHITE (OR ½ OZ WHIPPED AQUAFABA)

TWIST OF LEMON

Add all the ingredients to a cocktail shaker. Shake without ice to emulsify the lemon, then add ice and shake again. Strain into a chilled martini glass or champagne coupe. Garnish with a lemon twist.

Even if you've never been fired by your dad or dumped at the party you threw for your boyfriend, everyone's had a bad day and taken their mind off it with a weekend of partying, right? This pink cocktail is perfect for letting go without going full "lost weekend in Vegas." It's fun, flirty, and easy to drink—but don't forget, that doesn't mean there won't be consequences . . .

LET'S GET SMASHED

INGREDIENTS

5–6 BERRIES (RASPBERRIES WORK BEST) 6–8 MINT LEAVES	1⅔ OZ BOURBON ¾ OZ LIME JUICE ⅔ OZ SIMPLE SYRUP (SEE PAGE 9)	WEDGE OF LIME SPRIG OF MINT

Gently muddle the raspberries and mint in the bottom of a cocktail shaker—go easy as too much smashing will bring out bitter flavors from the mint leaves. Add the bourbon, lime juice, simple syrup, and ice. Shake and strain into an ice-filled tumbler. Garnish with a lime wedge or a mint sprig (or both!).

It's wedding season! And you don't have to go to absurd lengths to crash this party. Whether you are as cynical as John and Jeremy, or you believe in everlasting love, this is the perfect drink with which to toast a summer of fancy frocks, terrible best man speeches, and that unavoidable feeling of your best pair of heels sinking into a soft lawn.

LADY IN A WHITE DRESS

INGREDIENTS

1⅔ OZ GIN	⅔ OZ TRIPLE SEC	TWIST OF LEMON
⅔ OZ LEMON JUICE	1 EGG WHITE (OR 1 OZ WHIPPED AQUAFABA; OPTIONAL)	

Add all the ingredients to a cocktail shaker. Shake without ice to emulsify the lemon, then add ice and shake again. Strain into a chilled goblet glass or champagne coupe. Garnish with lemon twist, and rush to catch the bouquet.

WINTER HEART-WARMERS

If a more dashing drink comes along to try to turn your head, don't be fooled by its easy charm. A dark 'n' stormy may be brooding, a little reserved and hard to get to know, but this is a cocktail that likes you just the way you are.

Bridget's Dark 'n' Stormy

INGREDIENTS

1⅔ OZ DARK RUM	½ OZ LIME JUICE	5 OZ GINGER BEER

Fill a highball glass with ice. Pour in the rum and lime juice,
then top with ginger beer to taste—use less ginger beer if you prefer
things a little stronger and more intense . . .

Have you ever wondered if you are . . . destined to drink this cocktail? Whether you think your choice of drink should be decided by the whims of fate, the vagaries of chance, or simply what happens to be in your liquor cabinet, at least remain open to the possibility of a life-changing encounter with this drink.

WHAT'S YOUR NAME?

INGREDIENTS

¾ OZ BOURBON
¾ OZ PLUM LIQUEUR
½ OZ LEMON JUICE

⅓ OZ AGAVE SYRUP
1⅔ OZ GINGER ALE

A SPLASH OF LAGER
TWIST OF LEMON

Add the bourbon, plum liqueur, lemon juice, and agave syrup to a cocktail shaker filled with ice. Shake well and strain into a goblet glass filled with ice. Top with the ginger ale and lager. Garnish with a single glove and lemon twist.

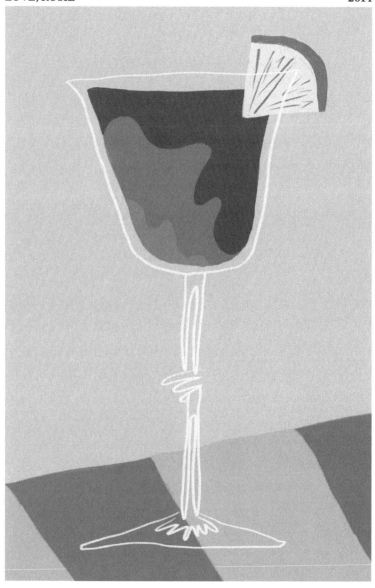

As we know from many rom-coms—and particularly this one—timing is everything, opportunities are easy to miss, and misunderstandings can get in the way. So don't let the chance to try this sweet but grown-up cocktail slip through your fingers. Yes, boy–girl friendships can be complicated, but fortunately, this cocktail is very simple.

LOVE FROM HARVARD

INGREDIENTS

2 OZ COGNAC	2–3 DASHES ANGOSTURA BITTERS	WEDGE OF ORANGE
²/₃ OZ SWEET VERMOUTH	CLUB SODA	

Fill a mixing glass with ice. Add the cognac, sweet vermouth, and bitters and stir until chilled. Strain into a tall goblet or wine glass, then top it up with around 1²/₃ ounces of club soda. Garnish with an orange wedge.

Sure, it's easy to be cynical. Maybe you want to write off this cocktail as a self-regarding drink that thinks a little too much of itself (why is there *egg*?!), but take some time away from the daily grind to get to know it, and just see what happens. Maybe Ryan Reynolds appears in a helicopter or—more fun—raps with Betty White in the woods.

THE NEW YORK SOUR

INGREDIENTS

1⅔ OZ WHISKEY, BOURBON, OR RYE	1 EGG WHITE (OR 1 OZ OF WHIPPED AQUAFABA)	½ OZ FULL-BODIED RED WINE
¾ OZ LEMON JUICE	2–3 DASHES ANGOSTURA BITTERS	WEDGE OF LEMON
½ OZ SIMPLE SYRUP (SEE PAGE 9)		

Add the whiskey, lemon juice, simple syrup, and egg white or aquafaba to a cocktail shaker. Shake without ice to emulsify the egg, then add ice and shake again. Strain into a rocks glass over ice and add the bitters. Then gently pour the red wine over the top, and garnish with a lemon wedge.

You could make this once or you could make it every day—that's up to you! It's a tiny bit sour at the start but it becomes sweet at the end, and that's what we want from a rom-com cocktail. This drink will remind you to always live in the moment. Plus, Punxsutawney Phil predicts that you will love it.

Greyhound Day

INGREDIENTS

1²/₃ OZ VODKA OR GIN (IT WORKS WITH EITHER!)

1²/₃ OZ PINK GRAPEFRUIT JUICE
1 TSP SIMPLE SYRUP (SEE PAGE 9)

SLICE OF GRAPEFRUIT

Add the vodka or gin, grapefruit juice, and simple syrup into an ice-filled cocktail shaker. Shake and strain into a tumbler filled with ice. Pop that grapefruit slice on the side and play the "Pennsylvania Polka."

If someone offers you a mansion in LA or a quaint cottage in the English countryside in which to spend Christmas, you'd be crazy to say no. If neither are offered, however, a classic Snowball should get you in the mood for a little festive romance. So dig around in the liquor cabinet for the Advocaat and prepare to obsess over "cottagecore." If you want to put a hankie on your face, that's entirely up to you.

HOUSESWAP SNOWBALL

INGREDIENTS

⅓ OZ LIME JUICE	3⅓ OZ LEMON-LIME SODA	MARASCHINO CHERRY
1⅔ OZ ADVOCAAT		

Fill a large balloon glass with ice. Add the lime juice followed by the Advocaat. Pour over the lemon-lime soda and stir gently. Garnish with a cherry.

On Wednesdays, we drink a Mean Martini. Or on any day, actually, because there are no stupid rules and Plastic cliques in this cocktail hour. So, don't worry about who's dating who, or if anyone is gossiping behind your back. Get your real friends together, and try this sweet and surprising twist on a Martini. Just watch out for that bin, there.

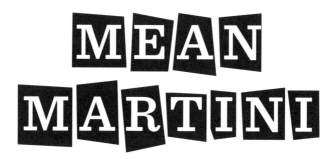

INGREDIENTS

1²/₃ OZ GIN	½ OZ LEMON JUICE	SLICE OF ORANGE
½ OZ COINTREAU	1 TSP ORANGE MARMALADE	

Add all the ingredients to a cocktail shaker filled with ice.
Shake hard and double strain into a chilled martini glass or
champagne coupe. Garnish with a slice of orange.

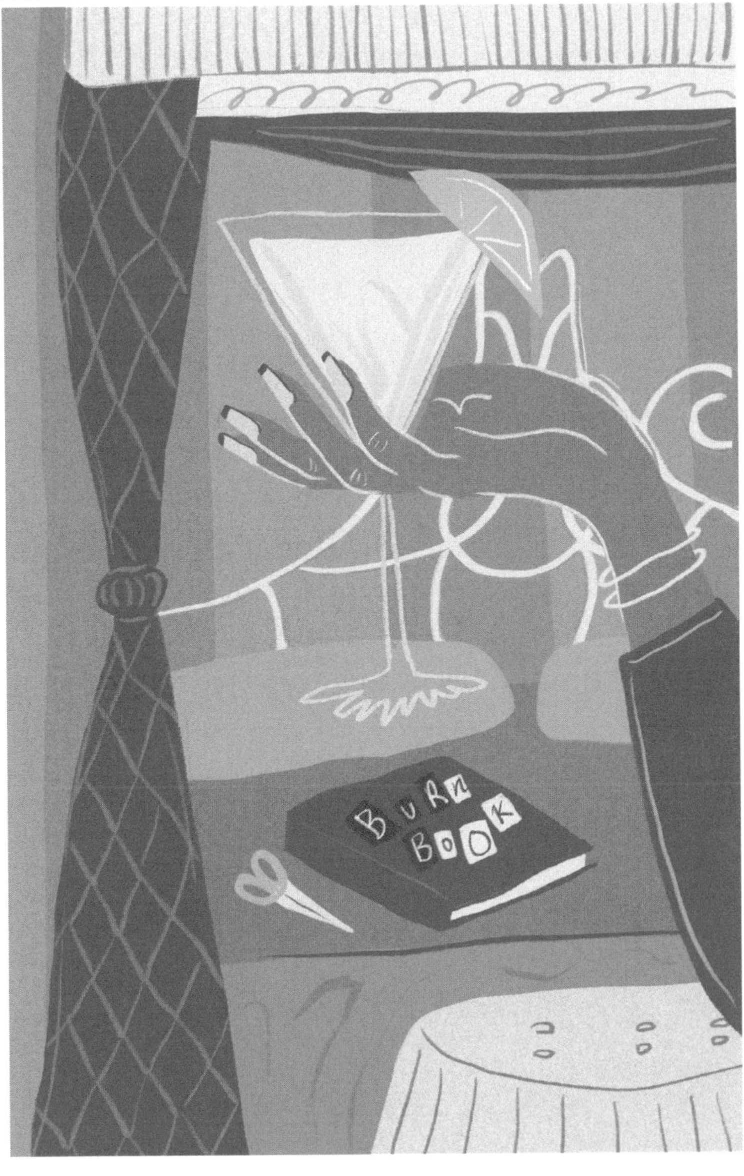
BURN
BOOK

It might seem crazy or far-fetched or like it just wouldn't work. But sometimes you just have to believe that you could mix wine, brandy, and fruit, and destiny will take care of the rest. Just like this Nora Ephron classic, in which the meet-cute happens at the end rather than the beginning of the movie, this drink breaks so many of the rules, but that makes us love it all the more.

SLEEPLESS IN SANGRIA

INGREDIENTS (SERVES 6)

2 ORANGES, CHOPPED
JUICE OF 1 LEMON
1 LEMON, CHOPPED

ONE 750 ML BOTTLE RIOJA (OR OTHER LIGHT RED SPANISH WINE)
3⅓ OZ BRANDY
¼ CUP SUPERFINE SUGAR

1 LB MIXED FRUIT (STRAWBERRIES, KIWIS, APPLES . . . WHATEVER YOU LIKE, REALLY), CHOPPED
12 OZ SPARKLING WATER

In a jug, muddle the chopped oranges, lemon juice, and chopped lemon and stir in the sugar. Then, pour in the red wine and brandy, stir, then refrigerate for at least two hours. Once chilled, stir in the chopped mixed fruit and sparkling water and serve in large ice-filled wine glasses or tumblers. Ideally at the top of the Empire State Building, but if this isn't an option, almost anywhere else will do.

TOP 3
MEG RYAN
ROM-COMS

1

SLEEPLESS IN SEATTLE

(1993)

2

YOU'VE GOT MAIL

(1998)

3

WHEN HARRY MET SALLY

(1989)

Why are people in rom-coms always going on dates to the opera? Next time the moon is full, why not try this tangy, gingery drink while listening to *La Bohème*—though it would probably feel less dramatic than Cher's incredible hair in this movie. (And yes, if you have always wondered, Nicolas Cage really was missing a tooth when he played Ronny.)

(MOSCOW) MULE-STRUCK

INGREDIENTS

1²⁄₃ OZ VODKA	GINGER BEER	SLICE OF LIME
JUICE OF ½ LIME	ANGOSTURA BITTERS (OPTIONAL)	SPRIG OF MINT

Add the vodka and lime juice to a highball glass or small punch cup and stir.
Fill with ice and top with ginger beer. You can add Angostura bitters, if you like an extra herby kick.
Garnish with a lime slice and mint sprig.

Travel back to the heady days of the late nineties, when the idea of two strangers meeting via the internet seemed kind of crazy. This is a grown-up cocktail that pairs perfectly with the smell of bookstores and a business rivalry with romantic potential . . .

YOU'VE GOT RUSTY NAIL

INGREDIENTS

1⅔ OZ SCOTCH WHISKEY	½ OZ DRAMBUIE	SLICE OF LEMON

Pour the Scotch whiskey and Drambuie into a short tumbler filled with ice and stir gently to combine. Garnish with a lemon slice and a copy of Jane Austen's *Pride and Prejudice* on the side.

Nothing says Christmas like Andrew Lincoln confessing his love to his best friend's wife, Colin Firth proposing to someone he's never had a conversation with, or Alan Rickman disappointing Emma Thompson. Like some of the plot points of *Love Actually*, an alcoholic drink made from egg, rum, and milk might seem a bit wrong, but it's all very sweet, perfectly Christmassy, and everything works out in the end.

EGGNOG ACTUALLY

INGREDIENTS (SERVES 10)

½ CUP SUPERFINE SUGAR	5 OZ DARK RUM	WHOLE NUTMEG
12 EGGS	1 QUART DOUBLE CREAM	CINNAMON STICK
12 OZ COGNAC	1 QUART WHOLE MILK	

This takes a little longer to make than most of the cocktails here, so it's best to make a batch for all the visitors who have heard you are watching *Love Actually* and want to come over. Take a large mixing bowl or punch bowl. Whisk the sugar into the eggs, then whisk in the cognac and rum. Add the cream and whisk again. Add the milk and whisk a final time. Ladle into ice-filled eggnog glasses and garnish each with a light sprinkle of freshly grated nutmeg. Add cinnamon sticks for an extra Christmassy flourish.

ROM-COM CHECKLIST

Consider yourself a rom-com connoisseur? Use this list of the greatest rom-coms of all time to keep track of how many you've seen, and how many cocktails you've drunk.

MOVIE	COCKTAIL
☐ *ROMAN HOLIDAY* (1953)	☐ RO-MANHATTAN HOLIDAY (PAGE 66)
☐ *BREAKFAST AT TIFFANY'S* (1961)	☐ BEE'S KNEES AT TIFFANY'S (PAGE 80)
☐ *SPLASH* (1984)	☐ TOM HANKY PANKY (PAGE 45)
☐ *MOONSTRUCK* (1987)	☐ (MOSCOW) MULE-STRUCK (PAGE 144)
☐ *WHEN HARRY MET SALLY* (1989)	☐ WHEN HARRY MET DAIQUIRI (PAGE 14)
☐ *PRETTY WOMAN* (1990)	☐ PALOMA WOMAN (PAGE 89)
☐ *GROUNDHOG DAY* (1993)	☐ GREYHOUND DAY (PAGE 135)
☐ *SLEEPLESS IN SEATTLE* (1993)	☐ SLEEPLESS IN SANGRIA (PAGE 141)
☐ *FOUR WEDDINGS AND A FUNERAL* (1994)	☐ FOUR WEDDINGS AND A FRENCH MARTINI (PAGE 112)
☐ *CLUELESS* (1995)	☐ CLUELESS COLADA (PAGE 17)
☐ *WHILE YOU WERE SLEEPING* (1995)	☐ CHICAGO COLLINS (PAGE 87)

MOVIE	COCKTAIL
☐ *PICTURE PERFECT* (1997)	☐ BOSTON BOUND (PAGE 77)
☐ *MY BEST FRIEND'S WEDDING* (1997)	☐ A CHAMPAGNE TOAST (PAGE 115)
☐ *THERE'S SOMETHING ABOUT MARY* (1998)	☐ THERE'S SOMETHING ABOUT (BLOODY) MARY (PAGE 52)
☐ *HOW STELLA GOT HER GROOVE BACK* (1998)	☐ STELLA'S GINGER BREW (PAGE 63)
☐ *SLIDING DOORS* (1998)	☐ SLIDING SLING (PAGE 90)
☐ *THE WEDDING SINGER* (1998)	☐ THE WEDDING SPRITZ (PAGE 106)
☐ *YOU'VE GOT MAIL* (1998)	☐ YOU'VE GOT RUSTY NAIL (PAGE 147)
☐ *10 THINGS I HATE ABOUT YOU* (1999)	☐ 10 THINGS I HATE ABOUT WOO WOO (PAGE 22)
☐ *NEVER BEEN KISSED* (1999)	☐ JOSIE'S JULEP (PAGE 38)
☐ *NOTTING HILL* (1999)	☐ NOTTING BELLINI (PAGE 70)
☐ *RUNAWAY BRIDE* (1999)	☐ BRIDE'S BRAMBLE (PAGE 117)
☐ *HIGH FIDELITY* (2000)	☐ HIGH(BALL) FIDELITY (PAGE 94)
☐ *WHAT HAPPENS IN VEGAS* (2008)	☐ LET'S GET SMASHED (PAGE 121)
☐ *LEGALLY BLONDE* (2001)	☐ ELLE SORORITY PRESIDENTE (PAGE 37)
☐ *AMERICA'S SWEETHEARTS* (2001)	☐ AMERICANO SWEETHEARTS (PAGE 75)
☐ *BRIDGET JONES' DIARY* (2001)	☐ BRIDGET'S DARK 'N' STORMY (PAGE 126)

MOVIE	COCKTAIL
☐ *SERENDIPITY* (2001)	☐ WHAT'S YOUR NAME? (PAGE 128)
☐ *SWEET HOME ALABAMA* (2002)	☐ SWEET HOME ALABAMA SLAMMER (PAGE 50)
☐ *MAID IN MANHATTAN* (2002)	☐ MAID'S MANHATTAN (PAGE 83)
☐ *HOW TO LOSE A GUY IN 10 DAYS* (2003)	☐ HOW TO LOSE A GIMLET IN 10 DAYS (PAGE 18)
☐ *LOVE ACTUALLY* (2003)	☐ EGGNOG ACTUALLY (PAGE 148)
☐ *13 GOING ON 30* (2004)	☐ MATTY-DOR (PAGE 33)
☐ *50 FIRST DATES* (2004)	☐ OOPSY (BRANDY) DAISY (PAGE 59)
☐ *ETERNAL SUNSHINE OF THE SPOTLESS MIND* (2004)	☐ ETERNAL TEQUILA SUNRISE OF THE SPOTLESS MIND (PAGE 78)
☐ *MEAN GIRLS* (2004)	☐ MEAN MARTINI (PAGE 138)
☐ *JUST LIKE HEAVEN* (2005)	☐ THE TENANT REVIVER (PAGE 25)
☐ *THE 40-YEAR-OLD VIRGIN* (2005)	☐ THE 40-YEAR-OLD VIRGIN MARGARITA (PAGE 103)
☐ *THE WEDDING DATE* (2005)	☐ NICK'S MARTINI (PAGE 104)
☐ *MR AND MRS SMITH* (2005)	☐ CONCEALED WEAPONS (PAGE 118)
☐ *WEDDING CRASHERS* (2005)	☐ LADY IN A WHITE DRESS (PAGE 122)
☐ *FAILURE TO LAUNCH* (2006)	☐ TRIPP SOUR (PAGE 34)
☐ *THE DEVIL WEARS PRADA* (2006)	☐ EL DESIGNER DIABLO (PAGE 93)

MOVIE	COCKTAIL
☐ *THE HOLIDAY* (2006)	☐ HOUSESWAP SNOWBALL (PAGE 136)
☐ *FORGETTING SARAH MARSHALL* (2008)	☐ FORGETTING SARAH MAI TAI (PAGE 42)
☐ *MAMMA MIA* (2008)	☐ MAMMA CUBA LIBRE (PAGE 56)
☐ *27 DRESSES* (2008)	☐ CHOOSE ME NEGRONI (PAGE 100)
☐ *THE UGLY TRUTH* (2009)	☐ MORNING SHOW FIZZ (PAGE 29)
☐ *500 DAYS OF SUMMER* (2009)	☐ 500 FLAVORS OF MOJITO (PAGE 49)
☐ *HE'S JUST NOT THAT INTO YOU* (2009)	☐ HE'S JUST NOT THAT INTO SEX ON THE BEACH (PAGE 60)
☐ *CONFESSIONS OF A SHOPAHOLIC* (2009)	☐ DITSY BRITZY SPRITZ (PAGE 84)
☐ *BRIDE WARS* (2009)	☐ A COSMOPOLITAN FEUD (PAGE 111)
☐ *THE PROPOSAL* (2009)	☐ THE NEW YORK SOUR (PAGE 132)
☐ *EASY A* (2010)	☐ EASY (A)MBROSIA (PAGE 26)
☐ *FLIPPED* (2010)	☐ RUM FLIPPED (PAGE 65)
☐ *CRAZY STUPID LOVE* (2011)	☐ CRAZY SHANDY LOVE (PAGE 21)
☐ *NO STRINGS ATTACHED* (2011)	☐ NO STRINGS BETWEEN THE SHEETS (PAGE 30)
☐ *ABOUT TIME* (2013)	☐ BACK IN TIME (PAGE 55)
☐ *LOVE, ROSIE* (2014)	☐ LOVE FROM HARVARD (PAGE 131)
☐ *ALWAYS BE MY MAYBE* (2019)	☐ ALWAYS BE MY MARTINI (PAGE 97)

153

CREDITS

I'LL HAVE WHAT SHE'S HAVING (pp 12-39) *When Harry Met Sally* (1989) directed by Rob Reiner, produced by Rob Reiner, Andrew Scheinman. *Clueless* (1995) directed by Amy Heckerling, produced by Scott Rudin, Robert Lawrence. *How to Lose a Guy in 10 Days* (2003) directed by Donald Petrie, produced by Lynda Obst, Robert Evans. *Crazy Stupid Love* (2011) directed by Glenn Ficarra and John Requa, produced by Eryn Brown, Steve Carell, Vance DeGeneres, Denise Di Novi, Jeffrey Harlacker, Charlie Hartsock and David Siegel. *10 Things I Hate About You* (1999) directed by Gil Junger, produced by Jeffrey Chernov, Jody Hedien, Andrew Lazar, Seth Jaret, Greg Silverman. *Just Like Heaven* (2005) directed by Mark Waters, produced by Laurie MacDonald, Walter F. Parkes, Marc Levy. *Easy A* (2010) directed by Will Gluck, produced by Zanne Devine, Will Gluck. *The Ugly Truth* (2009) directed by Robert Luketic, produced by Gary Lucchesi, Tom Rosenberg. *No Strings Attached* (2011) directed by Ivan Reitman, produced by Ivan Reitman, Joe Medjuck, Jeffrey Clifford. *13 Going on 30* (2004) directed by Gary Winick, produced by Susan Arnold, Gina Matthews, Donna Arkoff Roth. *Failure to Launch* (2006) directed by Tom Dey, produced by Scott Aversano, Ron Bozman, Karen Dexter and Scott Rudin. *Legally Blonde* (2001) directed by Robert Luketic, produced by Marc E. Platt, Ric Kidney. *Never Been Kissed* (1999) directed by Raja Gosnell, produced by Drew Barrymore, Jeffrey Downer, Sandy Isaac, Nancy Juvonen. **SUMMER OF LOVE (pp 40-67)** *Forgetting Sarah Marshall* (2008) directed by Nicholas Stoller, produced by Judd Apatow, Shauna Robertson. *Splash* (1984) directed by Ron Howard, produced by Brian Grazer, Ron Howard. *Flipped* (2010), directed by Rob Reiner, produced by Rob Reiner, Alan Greisman. *500 Days of Summer* (2009) directed by Marc Webb, produced by Mason Novick, Jessica Tuchinsky. *Sweet Home Alabama* (2002) directed by Andy Tennant, produced by Neal H. Moritz, Stokely Chaffin. *About Time* (2013) directed by Richard Curtis, produced by Tim Bevan, Eric Fellner. *There's Something About Mary* (1998) directed by Peter Farrelly, Bobby Farrelly, produced by Frank Beddor, Michael Steinberg. *Mamma Mia* (2008) directed by Phyllida Lloyd, produced by Judy Craymer, Gary Goetzman. *50 First Dates* (2004) directed by Peter Segal, produced by Jack Giarraputo, Steve Golin, Nancy Juvonen. *He's Just Not That Into You* (2009) directed by Ken Kwapis, produced by Nancy Juvonen, Drew Barrymore. *How Stella Got Her Groove Back* (1998) directed by Kevin Rodney Sullivan, produced by Deborah Schindler. *Roman Holiday* (1953) directed by William Wyler, produced by William Wyler. **DOWNTOWN DRINKS (pp 68-97)** *Notting Hill* (1999) directed by Roger Michell, produced by Duncan Kenworthy. *America's Sweethearts* (2001) directed by Joe Roth, produced by Billy Crystal, Susan Arnold, Donna Arkoff Roth. *Picture Perfect* (1997) directed by Glenn Gordon Caron, produced by Erwin Stoff. *Eternal Sunshine of the Spotless Mind* (2004) directed by Michel Gondry, produced by Anthony Bregman, Steve Golin. *Breakfast at Tiffany's* (1961) directed by Blake Edwards, produced by Martin Jurow, Richard Shepherd. *Maid in Manhattan* (2002) directed by Wayne Wang, produced by Elaine Goldsmith-Thomas, Jennifer Lopez. *Confessions of a Shopaholic* (2009) directed by P.J. Hogan, produced by Jerry Bruckheimer. *While You Were Sleeping* (1995) directed by Jon Turteltaub, produced by Roger Birnbaum, Joe Roth. *Pretty Woman* (1990) directed by Garry Marshall, produced by Arnon Milchan, Steven Reuther. *Sliding Doors* (1998) directed by Peter Howitt, produced by Sydney Pollack, Philippa Braithwaite. *The Devil Wears Prada* (2006) directed by David Frankel, produced by Wendy Finerman. *High Fidelity* (2000) directed by Stephen Frears, produced by Tim Bevan, Rudd Simmons, John Cusack. *Always Be My Maybe* (2019) directed by Nahnatchka Khan, produced by Nathan Kahane, Erin Westerman. **TIPPLES TO SAY I DO TO (pp 98-123)** *27 Dresses* (2008) directed by Anne Fletcher, produced by Roger Michell, Jonathan Clickman, Becki Cross Trujillo, Michael Mayer, Robert F. Newmyer, Erin Stam and Gary Barber. *The 40-Year-Old Virgin* (2005) directed by Judd Apatow, produced by Judd Apatow, Steve Carell, Andrew Jay Cohen, Jon Poll, Shauna Robertson, Seth Rogen, Clayton Townsend. *The Wedding Date* (2005) directed by Clare Kilner, produced by Jessica Bendinger, Mairi Bett, Paul Brooks, Michelle Chydzik Sowa, Jeff Levine, Nathalie Marciano, Scott Niemeyer, Jim Reeve, Steve Robbins, Norm Waitt. *The Wedding Singer* (1998) directed by Tim Herlihy, produced by Richard Brener, Jack Giarraputo, Brad Grey, Ira Shuman, Robert Simonds, Sandy Wernick, Brian Witten. *Bride Wars* (2009) directed by Gary Winick produced by Jay Cohen, Jonathan Filley, Kate Hudson, Matt Luber, Tony Ludwig, Arnon Milchan, Alan Riche, Devon Wilson, Julie Yorn. *Four Weddings and a Funeral* (1994) directed by Mike Newell, produced by Duncan Kenworthy, Tim Bevan, Richard Curtis, Eric Fellner. *My Best Friend's Wedding* (1997) directed by P.J.Hogan, produced by Ron Bass, Gil Netter, Patricia Whitcher, Jerry Zucker. *Runaway Bride* (1999) directed by Garry Marshall, produced by Tom Rosenberg, Ted Field, Robert W. Cort, Scott Kroopf, James Murray, Kevin Susman, Mario Iscovich, Gary Lucchesi, David Madden, Ellen H. Schwartz, Karen Stirgwolt, Ted Tannebaum, Richard S. Wright. *Mr and Mrs Smith* (2005) directed by Doug Liman, produced by Arnon Milchan, Akiva Goldsman, Lucas Foster, Patrick Wachsberger, Eric Mcleod Dawn Carter Erik Feig Lucas Foster Akiva Goldsman, Kim H. Winther. *What Happens in Vegas* (2008) directed by Tom Vaughan, produced by Michael Aguilar, Joe Caracciolo Jr, Dean Georgaris,Shawn Levy, Tom McNulty, Arnon Milchan, Jimmy Miller. *Wedding Crashers* (2005) directed by David Dobkin, produced by Peter Abrams, Cale Boyter, Richard Brener, Toby Emmerich, Robert L. Levy, Andrew Panay, Guy Riedel. **WINTER HEART WARMERS (pp 124-149)** *Bridget Jones' Diary* (2001) directed by Sharon Maguire, produced by Tim Bevan, Jonathan Cavendish, Liza Chasin, Eric Fellner, Helen Fielding, Debra Hayward, Peter McAleese. *Serendipity* (2001) directed by Peter Chelsom, produced by Peter Abrams, Robbie Brenner, Simon Fields, Julie Goldstein, Amy J. Kaufman, Robert L. Levy, Bob Osher, Andrew Panay, Amy Slotnick. *Love, Rosie* (2014) directed by Christian Ditter, produced by Simon Brooks, Don Carmody, James Flynn, Robert Kulzer, Jonnie Malachi, Martin Moszkowicz, Bernhard Thür. *The Proposal* (2009) directed by Anne Fletcher, produced by David Hoberman, Todd Lieberman. *Groundhog Day* (1993) directed by Harold Ramis, produced by Trevor Albert, Harold Ramis. *The Holiday* (2006) directed by Nancy Myers, produced by Bruce A. Block, Jennifer Eatz, Suzanne Farwell, Nancy Meyers. *Mean Girls* (2004) directed by Mark Waters, produced by Lorne Michaels. *Sleepless in Seattle* (1993), directed by Nora Ephron, produced by Gary Foster, Nora Ephron. *Moonstruck* (1987) directed by Norman Jewison, produced by Norman Jewison, Bonnie Palef, Patrick J. Palmer. *You've Got Mail* (1998) directed by Nora Ephron, produced by Nora Ephron, Lauren Shuler Donner. *Love Actually* (2003) directed by Richard Curtis produced by Tim Bevan, Liza Chasin, Eric Fellner, Debra Hayward, Duncan Kenworthy, Chris Thompson.

155

INDEX

First published in 2024 by Pop Press,
an imprint of Ebury Publishing

Printed in the United States of America
First America Edition 2025

For information about permission to
reproduce selections from this book, write
to Permissions, Countryman Press, 500 Fifth
Avenue, New York, NY 10110

For information about special discounts
for bulk purchases, please contact
W. W. Norton Special Sales at
specialsales@wwnorton.com or 800-233-4830

Manufacturing by Versa Press
Book design by Evi-O.Studio, Katherine Zhang
Illustrations: Evi-O.Studio, Katherine Zhang,
Siena Zadro
Production manager: Devon Zahn

Countryman Press
www.countrymanpress.com

An imprint of W. W. Norton & Company, Inc.
500 Fifth Avenue, New York, NY 10110
www.wwnorton.com

ISBN: 978-1-68268-980-6

1 2 3 4 5 6 7 8 9 0